Eliminate the IRS

With

A 5% flat income tax

By Ralph Sweitzer

I0435706

Preface

The politicians in Washington are using the IRS to harass and intimidate Americans. Over the years the IRS has become bloated and is used by politicians of both parties as a political weapon. There are over 74,000 pages of regulations in the current federal tax code. This gives the IRS tremendous power over the American people. Soon under the Affordable Care Act known as Obama Care the IRS will have your medical records along with your financial records. The founding fathers never intended government to have this much power. This is the very tyranny they fought against in the revolutionary war. The current tax code inhibits robust economic growth. This book describes a simple plan to dramatically reduce the intrusive power of government and create a robust economy.

Currently this country is in a real financial mess. The national debt is over $17 trillion dollars as of this writing and the Gross Domestic Product (GDP) is growing at an anemic 1.5% a year. The budget deficit has been over a trillion dollars for the last 4 years and the national debt keeps growing.

Unemployment is stuck at an all time high with more people out of work than ever before with no chance of an economic recovery. Housing sales and prices are also down. More than 70% of the people think the nation is headed in the wrong direction.

Our national defenses are down and our foreign policy is in a mess mainly because as a nation we're broke. Our national debt is greater than our GDP. We don't have any money to really do anything.

There is gridlock in our nation's capital. One party wants to spend the country into oblivion and raise taxes while the other party wants to slash all spending. More than 51 million people are on food stamps. And now we have our most powerful agency, the IRS intimidating and spying on law abiding Americans. The IRS is the very tyranny our founders fought against in the revolutionary war. This can all be easily fixed.

President John Kennedy had a famous quote.

"Our problems are manmade--therefore, they can be solved by man. And man can be as big as he wants. No problem of human destiny is beyond human beings. Man's reason and spirit have often solved the seemingly unsolvable--and we believe they can do it again."

I wrote this book to provide a solution to our problems. To become the once great nation we used to be. A very simple solution to end the IRS tyranny, reduce the size of government and supercharge the U.S. economy so every person in this country can realize the American dream.

We got ourselves into this mess and like President Kennedy said we can get ourselves out of this mess. The way to get out of this mess is to grow the economy. It will take as they say "thinking outside of the box" to do it.

By reading this book you'll see just how easy and simple it is.

Table of Contents

Chapter 1

Big Brother is watching YOU!

In light of the recent IRS scandals that have rocked the nation there is a more urgent need for a true flat tax for everyone who earns income in this country. The IRS has become more than a tax collection agency. It has become a means to intimidate political opponents and suppress freedom of expression. President Richard Nixon used the IRS to intimidate his political opponents. Other presidents have done it as well such as Presidents Lyndon Johnson and now Barack Obama.

This agency has the power to destroy anyone it wants through relentless pressure and intimidation. It has the power to put the person or group into financial ruin and in many cases put them in prison. It's the U.S. version of the Nazi Gestapo or Soviet KGB. As a free country or a country that claims to be free this agency is not in line with the freedoms guaranteed by the constitution.

The power of the IRS is intrusive to every freedom loving American. It has the ability to look into all of your financial affairs and very soon your personal health records. They can garnish your wages, seize bank accounts and pensions, close businesses and even put you into prison. In many ways the IRS is like the Mafia. If they feel you owe them back taxes they can impose loan sharking like interest rates and penalties on you without due process of law. Like the Mafia they will be relentless pursuing you. There are special tax courts that usually side with the IRS thus making a fair and impartial trial impossible. There is no due process of law when dealing with the IRS. Immediately you're deemed guilty and you will have to spend a fortune to prove you're innocent.

This agency is truly "Big Brother" from George Orwell's book called 1984. In the book Big Brother is involved with every aspect of your life. Big Brother watched and listened to every person in the country. Now with the Affordable Care Act or rather known as Obama Care the IRS will be intruding into your health care along with all your financial income. Why do think the Obama administration pushed so hard to get our medical records computerized? Not for lowering medical cost as they claimed. It will be for one more level of snooping on Americans. When Obama Care is fully implemented you'll have to get your health care provider and insurance coverage approved by the IRS. Between the IRS and Health and Human Services (HHS) agency there will be no privacy or freedom with your heath care.

The IRS along with the Justice Department has all the guns and all the money to take away your freedoms and ruin your life. You have no say so but to pay up, shut up or be destroyed.

Chapter 2

Who works for Who?

As Americans we're lead to believe the government works for the people. This is a joke and couldn't be further from the truth. As far as the government is concerned we work for them. This whole concept has gone upside down. In the Constitution the founding fathers wanted the government to work for the people. Today, unfortunately the people are servants to the government at all levels. In the past 200 plus years something went terribly wrong. The government has gotten so large and intrusive in our everyday lives our liberties are being steadily eroded.

Currently the government through the IRS knows all of your finances. Where you make your money and where you spend it. By law you must report to the government what you make and where you made it. You even have to report where you spent your money to get a tax deduction. When Obama Care gets fully implemented through the "so called" Affordable Care Act the government through the IRS will know what health provider you have. They'll have access to your computerized medical records. Contrary to what they're saying your finances and medical records will be shared by government agencies. The abuse of power in this country is rampant. The government through the Health and Human Services agency will determine if you get certain life saving medical treatments based on your age and other health factors. In Obama Care the provision for the Independent Payment Advisory Board (IPAB) or as former governor Sarah Palin called "death panel" is made up of 15 members appointed by the president to achieve savings in Medicare. This means the government will analyze the cost / benefit ratio of a senior's treatment. Even if you're in good health at 85 and run 4 miles a day you could be denied treatment by this panel just because of your age. Wait till the panel realizes you may be affiliated with the opposition party. Your treatment will be denied if you want it paid for by Medicare. Because they'll have all your financial and medical records the government can now "means" test you. The IPAB may rule you have the financial means to pay for treatment yourself rather than Medicare.

The government now tracks all of our emails, phone texts and phone calls. The government tracks all of our financial transactions. The government wants to know our buying habits. What kind of light bulbs we buy and what we set our thermostats to. The government wants to know what kind of car we buy. We could be punished with a carbon tax if we don't buy an approved vehicle. The government will begin to track your doctor visits. Remember computerized medical records!

Does this sound like a government who works for the people?

To the federal government there are two economies. The first is the general economy that you and I know and live in. There are large and small companies doing commerce with each other. There are hard working people going to work every day and living their lives. The federal government thinks of itself as a separate economy or even a separate country. The federal government wants people to go to work, earn money and pay taxes to feed its economy. The federal and state governments have all the guns. They can use those guns on the people in the real economy to extract wealth without having to work for it. The real economy is innovative, builds and develops things like buildings, computers, aircraft, cars, etc. The real economy provides services such as communications, transportation, agriculture, etc. The real economy builds wealth. The government economy steals through the tax code at a point of a gun the wealth created by the real economy. The government economy does not innovate or create wealth. Contrary to popular belief the government does not create jobs. The real economy does. The people in the real economy are subjects or servants to the government economy because the government has all the guns and can steal the wealth at will.

It wasn't supposed to be this way. The founding fathers never intended for the government to steal wealth from the people. In fact the Revolutionary War was fought because the King's government was stealing wealth from the people in America at the point of a gun through taxation.

The size and scope of the U.S. government and its ability to steal wealth from the people at a point of a gun is huge by comparison anything the King of England did. The whole purpose of fighting the Revolutionary War was to eliminate what we currently have now.

Employees from federal, state and even local governments think the people work for them and it is our duty and obligation to feed the government machine through taxation.

If you don't think the government has all the guns try not paying your so called "voluntary" taxes. You'll see those guns and they'll be pointing at you.

After stealing your money the government wastes and squanders it. Your money is sent to hostile governments in the form of "foreign aid. That's right; people who hate us receive your tax money. Many government agencies take extravagant junkets or "conferences" as they call it at tax payer's expense. The GAO spent millions of tax payer's dollars on lavish conferences in Las Vegas. The IRS has spent over $50 million dollars on lavish "conferences". You can't do anything about it because they have all the guns and all the power. Just to illustrate the fact, did you know the Department of Education (DOE) has a SWAT team equipped with automatic weapons to crash in the doors of students who can't pay their student loans? We work for them. They are the plantation owners and the tax payers are their slaves. At anytime one of these government agencies can come down on you and destroy your life. That's especially true with the IRS.

With the IRS, EPA, Department of Labor, DOJ, DHS we currently have tyranny. The kind of tyranny our founding fathers fought against. If any of these agencies doesn't like something about you or what you have to say exercising your right to free speech they can make life for you a living hell. There are so many laws and regulations in this country hanging over our heads you never know when you're breaking one of them. Also agencies like the IRS can interpret laws anyway they want to suit their political needs.

It wasn't meant to be this way. The founding fathers of the United States did not want a centralized government with all that power imposing its will on the people. The founding fathers purposely wanted a de-centralized government where power was concentrated in the states and the people. Originally, when the union was formed the federal government was not allowed to levy and collect income taxes on the people. The federal government could only levy interstate tariffs and excise taxes. As goods traveled from state to state a tax could be collected by the federal government. The states had all the power. Each state could levy and collect income taxes on its local population. The people could vote for members of the House of Representatives but each state legislature appointed two senators to the U.S. Senate. The interest of the people was represented by the House of Representatives and the interest of the states was represented by the Senate. The states and the people had all the power and the federal government had very little.

All that changed with the 16th and 17th amendments to the constitution in 1913. The 16th amendment allowed the federal government to levy and collect income taxes. The 17th amendment allowed the population to vote for each of the two senators from each state.

The 16th amendment known as the Revenue Act of 1913 gave birth to the Internal Revenue Service (IRS). The major industrialist and capitalist of the time such as John D. Rockefeller, J.P Morgan and Andrew Carnegie wanted power to be shifted from the states and concentrated in the federal government. This way it was easier for them to influence the government via crony capitalism if power was concentrated in one place. Men such as these fought very hard with their influence and wealth to have the Revenue Act of 1913 passed and ratified in the Constitution. They knew that by its passage it was good for their businesses and allowed them to increase their wealth and influence. They also knew that a more powerful federal government would bring more business their way. To collect the taxes with the new power of the federal government there needed to be an agency to do this. The Internal Revenue Service (IRS) was created for that purpose. At first the income taxes were just on the very wealthy and were very low like 2%. At first it was more of a voluntary system. But as time went on congress gave the IRS more and broader powers. They gave them the power to collect taxes, intimidate, seize, fine, levy heavy interest rates and even imprison through "stacked deck" tax courts.

The argument for the 17th amendment was monopolies such as Standard Oil and J.P. Morgan could no longer manipulate and influence state legislatures who appointed senators. But in reality because of an uninformed voting population their influence could be more easily concentrated and focused at the federal level instead of each state.

With these two amendments there was a major power shift from the states to the federal government. These two amendments rendered the states powerless and the federal government all powerful. With these two amendments the power was mainly put into the hands of the executive branch of the federal government, the president.

In the constitution the president was meant to be a servant of the congress. The president was to carry out the will of the congress. The president was the executor of the laws passed by congress. That's why it's called the executive branch of government.

With the 16th and 17th amendments the president is more like a king than an executor or servant of the congress. Much of the founding fathers "checks and balance" was eroded with those two amendments. With these two amendments to the Constitution the president in the executive branch went from a servant or executor of the congress to being supreme over the congress. The executive branch controls the very agencies in the government that erode our freedoms and create tyranny. The larger the executive branch grows the more power it has.

Chapter 3

Feed the beast

In 1913 when the 16th amendment was ratified the U.S. GDP was $65 billion dollars. Just one hundred years later in 2013 it's grown to $16 trillion dollars or nearly 250 times. In 1913 the federal budget was $714 million dollars with a $1 million dollar deficit. Just one hundred years later in 2013 the budget has grown to $3.7 trillion dollars with a $1.5 trillion dollar deficit. In 1913 the executive branch had seven departments. In 2013 there are 15 departments each requiring massive amounts of tax payer revenue.

In 2013 there are nearly 5 million federal employees. To put this into perspective, there are more federal employees than the population of the countries of Ireland or Costa Rica. There are as many people employed by the federal government as the population of the country Norway.

Here is the breakdown of federal spending in 1913.

Federal Pensions:	$0
Federal Health Care:	$5 million
Federal Education:	$8 million
National Defense:	$427 million
Federal Welfare:	$7 million

Compare that to federal spending 100 years later in 2013.

Federal Pensions:	$749 billion
Federal Health Care:	$820 billion
Federal Education:	$140 billion
National Defense:	$847 billion
Federal Welfare:	$397 billion

By 2013, just 100 years later the federal budget has grown almost 5 times in size it was in 1913.

Some of the growth has been due to inflation. Some of the growth has been due to national defense to fight World War 1, World War 2 and the cold war but most of it has been has been due to special interest group and party politics.

In 1913 the federal tax code was only 400 pages. Just 100 years later the current federal tax code is almost 74,000 pages. The current 74,000 pages of tax code are made up of vague laws and regulations influenced by special interest groups and party politics.

Some of the tax code is so vague it has to be interpreted by IRS bureaucrats. Depending on which political party is in power the tax code can be interpreted in various ways. This happens when congress passes a tax law it's mostly in principal. It's left up to the bureaucrats at the IRS to interpret what congress meant or their 'intent' and gets enforced in any way they want. With 74,000 pages of tax law there can be many interpretations and opinions by the bureaucrats running the IRS.

The same applies to the EPA, HHS and other departments. Currently the HHS department is interpreting the massive Affordable Health Care law known as Obama Care. The IRS is also interpreting Obama Care into law. Currently the HHS interpretation is over 20,000 pages.

The federal government is so massive and over reaching the problem is only going to get worse unless congress can do something about it. I don't dispute the need for taxes. Taxes pay for many government services such as a strong defense, interstate highway system, air traffic control system, land and water management, environmental protection and a host of other government services. Taxes also inhibit the economy from growing. There is an old saying "if you want to stop something just tax it". The current tax code actually inhibits economic growth. The tax code is so complicated IRS bureaucrats can pick and chose who gets exemptions and who doesn't. Who qualifies and gets a tax free status and who doesn't. And if a bureaucrat has a personal political leaning they might be lenient on one person or organization of the same political leaning and harsh on another person or group they politically disagree with. Congressmen and Senators contact the IRS routinely to look into a groups or individuals that have different political views.

There is too much power in the hands of the IRS and its thousands of bureaucrats. Power has to taken away from the IRS. This can be done with a much simpler and fair tax code. A fair and simple tax code will end political influence.

We need a tax code that allows U.S. economy to grow at a robust pace. We need a tax code that is fair to all Americans regardless of political ideology or party. We need a tax code that Americans have no fear of the agency that collects those taxes.

We need a tax code that is fair to all Americans with everyone paying their fair share. Currently 47% of all citizens pay no income taxes while the remaining 53% pay all the taxes. This isn't fair because 100% of our citizens use the services provided by taxes.

Chapter 4

So How Do We Eliminate the IRS?

As mentioned before the current tax code is 74,000 pages of often vague interpretable regulations. The IRS has over 106,000 employees and a federal budget of over $12 billion dollars a year. That number of IRS employees is needed to manage the massive over bearing tax code.

What is needed is a simple flat tax on all forms of income.

- A simple flat tax that could provide explosive economic growth in the U.S.
- A tax code that could reduce the number of IRS employees from 106,000 to 10,000 and an annual budget of around $500 million.
- A tax code that could reduce the number of pages from 74,000 to 1,000.

I'm proposing a 5%flat income tax on all forms of income such as earned wages, capital and corporate profits.

Everyone in this country that earns income of any form should pay taxes. In this country there are very fortunate wealthy people and less fortunate poor people. Regardless of source of income everyone should pay taxes at the same 5% rate. Under this proposal there would be no deductions, exemptions, tax credits or loop holes of any kind.

I picked a 5% flat income tax for very good reasons.

- **No one wants to raise taxes on the poor.** As I mentioned about 47% of the population pay no income tax at all. A 5% flat tax is almost no tax at all. If a young person in high school works for a fast food restaurant and gets paid $100 a week then he or she would pay $5.00 in federal taxes and take home $95.00. Note that same person is already subject to a 6.2% flat tax known as FICA.

- **The rich or wealthy would also pay their fair share at the income tax rate of 5%.** If a person earned by wages or capital gains $1million dollars a year they would pay $50,000 in taxes. They would not be able to use fancy accountants or CPAs to find legal loop holes to evade paying taxes. The current 74,000 tax code is full of legal loop holes to evade taxes. That can't be done under this plan.

- **Corporations would also pay their fare share at the 5% income tax rate on net profits.** Large and small businesses would pay the same rate. Corporate net profits would have to determine after business expenses. A few years ago General Electric (GE) paid no income taxes on $12 billion in net profit. Using the current 74,000 page tax code their accountants at big CPA firms were able to find special write offs and legal loop holes to evade paying any taxes. With the plan I'm proposing GE would have paid $600 million in taxes to the federal government. Business expense determination would be very simple. If the business had to spend money to make money it could be deducted from gross profits. There would be no more special tax credits or exemptions the large oil companies currently get with the existing tax code. No more special tax breaks or tax credits to favored industries such as solar energy companies and electric automobiles.

- **Capital gains would be taxed at 5%.** Investments into the financial markets would sky rocket. Investments from around the globe would pour into U.S. financial markets. Currently the capital gains tax rate is 15%. At the current capital gains tax rate, if you bought 1000 shares of stock at $5.00 a share and 2 years later you sold the stock at $10.00 a share you will pay $750 in tax.

  With a capital gains tax of 5%, if you bought 1000 shares of a stock at $5.00 a share and 2 years later sold the stock for $10.00 a share you would pay $250 in taxes. Your tax burden would be reduced by 66%. Under the current capital gains tax rate of 15%, if you bought a house for $250,000 and 5 years later sold it for $350,000 your tax burden would be $15,000. With a capital gains tax of 5% your tax burden would be $5,000. That's significant.

- **The current business tax rate is 35%.** If a business made $1 million dollars in profit their current tax burden is $350,000.

- **Low taxes mean more jobs.** If the same business has a 5% flat corporate / business tax it would only pay $50,000 in federal taxes. That's $300,000 savings that same business can use to buy equipment or expand their work force to create additional jobs.

- **No taxes on Social Security benefits.** Currently Social Security recipients have to pay taxes on what they receive from the government. In 1993 taxes of Social Security benefits were raised. In the 5% flat tax being proposed there would be no taxes levied on Social Security, welfare or any other federal or state aid. Only income from earned wages, capitals gains and corporate profits would be taxed at a 5% flat rate.

- **Everyone should pay taxes.** We all use the services taxes pay for such as the interstate highway system, air traffic control system, military protection, federal and state law enforcement, etc. If we all use these services provided by our government then why shouldn't everyone who earns income pay some small amount of taxes. It's called having "skin in the game" or a "stake in the game".

- **No deductions, exemptions, credits or loop holes.** The 5% flat tax being proposed eliminates all deductions, exemptions and loop holes. In the current 74,000 page tax code tax payers need to take these deductions, exemptions, credits or loop holes to lower their tax burden. No need to do that with a 5% flat tax. Practically no tax rate at all.

- **Only religious organizations would be exempt.** If you're not a religious organization such as a church, Jewish synagogue, Muslim Mosque and you receive money then you would be subject to the 5% income tax. Unions would have to pay and not be exempt.

- **Take the politics out of the tax code.** With this plan the IRS could not be pressured or persuaded by Senators or Congressmen to look at people or organizations that differ with them politically. Every person, business and organization would be at the same simple tax rate and play by the same rules.

Chapter 5

The benefits of this plan

A 5% flat tax on earned wages, capital gains and corporate and business profits would be great for the U.S. economy. The U.S. economy is consumer driven. The more money in circulation benefits the economy. The more money in consumer's pocket the more they will spend into the economy.

- Currently under the oppressive 74,000 page tax code if a family earns $100,000 Adjusted Gross Income (AGI) and has the usual deductions of children, mortgage, property taxes, etc. they will pay about 21% in federal taxes. That is $21,000 in taxes after deductions. They'll only get to keep $79,000. Why do they take all those deductions? To reduce their tax burden.

- **More money in your pocket.** If that same family pays just 5% flat tax with no deductions proposed under this plan they would only pay $5,000 in federal tax. They get to keep an extra $16,000. They would put that money back into the economy by buying furniture, automobiles, a larger house, and clothes for the kids, home improvements, etc.

- **The U.S. economy will boom.** The economy will see job growth like it has never seen before. The U.S. will be more competitive in the world market. The U.S. economy will dominate the world markets.

- Small and large business will pay significantly less taxes thus seeing greater profits. The result will be more spending by businesses and **more jobs created**. The unemployment rate will probably fall between 2% - 3.5% because of the increased job growth.

- The federal government will see greatly increased tax receipts because of the economic boom. People and businesses will have more money to spend and the "velocity of money" changing hands will go off the charts.

- State and local governments will also benefit with the increased job growth, economic activity though state income and sales taxes.

- With increased tax receipts caused by the economic boom the deficit will go to surplus and the national debts could be reduced.

- With the greatly expanding economy causing much more job growth people will be able to get off of public assistance. Most people don't want a handout from the government. They want a job.

- **Less government.** About 90% of the IRS can be eliminated with this tax plan. Most people in this country receive earned wages from an employer. Under this plan the employer deducts 5% from the employee's gross pay and sends it into the federal government. The employee doesn't have to keep track of deductions, tax credits or other things like that. At the IRS the bureaucrats don't need to qualify a deduction because there are no deductions under this plan. Filing taxes will be very simple for most people. There will be no refunds or owing taxes because it has already been paid to the government at the time of receiving the paycheck through payroll withholding.

- **The Social Security fund will benefit.** With increased jobs there will be increased receipts going into the Social Security trust fund.

- **Social programs will prosper.** Programs like Medicare and Medicaid will reap the benefits of a 5% flat tax on every kind of income. As previously mentioned the U.S. economy will boom with increase economic activity and increased revenues into the federal government. All social programs will benefit.

- **Increased defense spending.**

Currently the U.S. has been cutting back on defense and development of new weapon systems. The current GDP is so pathetic it has caused massive budget deficits and politicians always look to cutting defense. With the increased GDP and tax revenues caused by a 5% flat tax on all forms of income defense spending can increase. Defense spending, readiness and a strong military are what keep our country free.

- **Increased GDP.**

Currently with 74,000 page tax code the U.S. annual GDP has been averaging about 1.5% which is pathetic. A 5% flat tax on all forms of income will unleash the U.S. economy.

Velocity of money changing hands will greatly increase. Expect an annual GDP growth rate between 5% - 7%.

Medicare will benefit

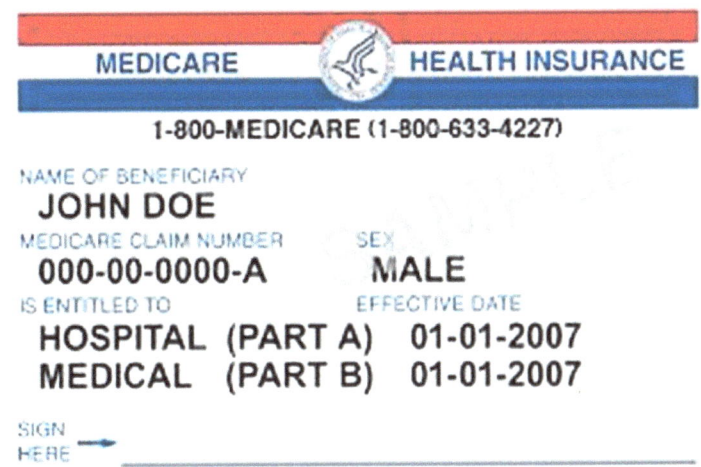

With increased job growth caused by the 5% flat tax on all forms of income there will be more people working. More people working means more people paying into the Medicare trust fund. Obama Care is looking for ways to limit Medicare costs by limiting payments to doctors who care for seniors on Medicare. The result will be limiting medical services to senior citizens. Currently there are not enough people making good wages to adequately fund the program. Low wage workers don't contribute enough through their paychecks to fund the system.

All that will change with this proposed flat income tax plan. As the economy greatly improves people in the work force will increase along with wages. Receipts into the Medicare fund will increase. Over the long run this plan will be able to save Medicare from bankruptcy.

More people graduating from college

With more money in circulating in an expanding economy there will be a greater demand for college educated workers. With the government collecting more tax revenue there will be more availability for Pell grants. In a robust economy people with more money will be able donate to their favorite college which turns into more scholarships. A more educated work force will keep the U.S. dominate as the number one economy in the world.

Chapter 6

The Nay Sayers

It will be argued that a 5% flat tax will cause massive budget deficits. Opponents to this plan will say the government won't be able to pay its bills, fund its departments and meet its obligations. I say nonsense to that. Nothing could be further from the truth. With all the extra money in circulation due to the 5% flat tax the government will be awash in tax revenue. Remember the old saying "if you want to stop something then tax it". The opposite holds true. Remove or lower taxes on something and it will flourish and take off.

Here is an example what happened when taxes were raised in the Omnibus Budget Reconciliation Act of 1990. There was a 30% excise tax placed on autos over $30,000, boats over $100,000, and firs over $10,000 and private planes over $250,000. The rich quit buying new boats, luxury cars, private planes and firs. The result was sales dramatically fell in these industries and they suffered great financial losses. Many of them went out of business and there were a lot of job losses. These extreme tax rates were ultimately dropped and the industries have rebounded.

There is also compelling evidence that reducing taxes on various occasions has taken the country out of recession. In 1962 the country was in recession and President John Kennedy argued for a massive reduction in taxes. Taxes were reduced but unfortunately he was not able to see the economic boom of the '60s. In 1981 President Ronald Reagan inherited a very bad recession. He immediately convinced congress to reduce taxes to stimulate the economy. It worked and caused the economic boom of the '80s which was one of the biggest in the history of the country.

In contrast, in 1929 the country suffered one of the biggest stock market plunges in U.S. history at that time. Initially it caused a mild recession. However, President Herbert Hoover immediately increased spending and raised taxes. That was the greatest contributor to the severe economic Great Depression of the 1930s. President Franklin Roosevelt continued with high taxes and the depression lasted for more than 13 years. Presidents Hoover and Roosevelt would have been wise to reduce taxes to stimulate the economy, get out of recession and eliminate the Great Depression.

Opponents to this plan will say it will hurt or destroy the CPA and accounting industry. Opponents will also say it will hurt the legal industry where it pertains to tax attorneys. Opponents will also say it will cause massive layoffs and job reductions at the IRS. Laws passed by congress should be for the benefit of all the U.S. citizens and not a select few. Laws should not be passed to create industries or provide financial favor to certain industries. Some of the current 74,000 page tax code is intended to prop up certain industries and create financial favors to others. It is also used as a political weapon by both political parties to inhibit, punish or prevent industries it doesn't like.

The Nay Sayers will say a 5% flat income tax with no deductions will hurt charitable contributions. I say they are wrong. The American people are very generous. With more money in their pockets thus creating a vibrant economy, charitable contributions will increase. It's a fact that during a recession charitable monetary contributions go down. Also charitable goods contributions go down. When people have more money to spend, charitable goods contributions such as clothing, furniture, vehicles, etc. increase because people will be buying more of these goods as replacements. They will give their old goods to charity.

Some Nay Sayers will argue this will hurt the real estate market because of no mortgage deductions. The opposite would be true because people will have more money in their pockets to afford higher priced homes and higher mortgages. The real estate market will boom. New and existing home sales will boom.

The Nay Sayers always point to the surplus during the second term of President Bill Clinton. President Clinton raised taxes higher than any president in history. During the first two years of the Clinton administration there was a recession and large budget deficits. The real truth is in 1995 when the Republicans took control of the congress they forced balanced budgets on the president and forced the lowering of the capital gains tax. This turned the economy around to an economic and stock market boom. Just imagine if income taxes were also lowered. Clinton would have no part of that.

Chapter 7

Corruption in government

The IRS is so large and the tax code is so big there is bound to be corruption. With the powers the congress has given the IRS over the years a corrupt president can order that political enemies be harassed and terrorized.

The majority of the current tax law is so vague that much of it is left up to interpretation by IRS bureaucrats. Our politicians also use the tax law to punish political opponents and give tax favors to political friends. Here is a perfect example. One party may favor big oil companies so the tax law is changed to give them tax credits. Another party in power may not favor big oil companies and use the tax laws to punish them. As an example in 2001 and 2005 President George W. Bush got congress to give big oil companies big tax credits. The president was friends with big oil. In 2008 President Barack Obama wanted to eliminate those tax credits and raise taxes on big oil companies. This president did not like big oil. Instead he gave tax credits to solar energy companies whom he liked. It's all politics but it hurts the country.

I doubt the authors of the 1913 Revenue Act wanted or envisioned the IRS would be used in a political way or as a political weapon.

It's not right to use the tax code for political favors to friends. It's not right to use the tax code to punish political enemies or individuals who disagree with the government.

Senators and congressman of both parties call on the IRS to investigate groups and individuals they disagree with. In this country we're supposed to have freedom of speech and expression. But lately freedom of speech is squashed by getting the IRS to open an investigation of a group or individual. Recently in 2013 it was disclosed the IRS was investigating groups that applied for 501C4 tax exemptions because the current administration disagreed with them politically. The agency dragged its feet for years without giving approval. Groups that were politically friendly with the administration got tax exempt status very quickly. The agency has been turned into a weapon for political power and corruption and it must stop.

 All this is eliminated with the 5% flat tax previously described. Everyone, every company pays and we all pay at the same rate – 5% on any kind of income. Because there is no tax deductions, tax credits, tax exemptions or loop holes it will be impossible to use this agency for any other purpose than to collect the nation's taxes.

The 5% flat tax plan described in this book removes the politics from the IRS.

Chapter 8

Is there a hidden agenda to limit the size of the U.S. economy?

There must be because anyone with common sense would reject the current tax code of 74,000 pages. What are the people in the U.S. Senate and House of Representatives smoking to put up with such a repressive and corrupt current tax code? Either the people we send to congress are very stupid or they are very corrupt to want the current tax code. They must like the power they hold over us with it. Is it possible many of them are high on prescription drugs and can't think logically or clearly? I think members of congress should disclose what medications they are taking. Certain medications could affect their logic, judgment and decision making that has an effect on all citizens of the U.S. If some of them are on certain anti-depressants their judgment is affected. Some of these drugs have "no driving" warnings on the label because judgment can be impaired. That should hold true for making decisions regarding laws that affects all of our lives too.

There should be punishment when congress passes a budget with a deficit. The percentage of deficit should be withheld from their paychecks.

Chapter 9

Let's save Social Security

Politicians keep talking about "saving Social Security" and never get around to doing it. Some of them come up with one hair brain idea after another such as means testing, raising the eligibility age and reducing benefits. None of these ideas will work and will cause hardships to people currently drawing Social Security or about to. Currently in 2013 if you make less than $113K a year you have to contribute to the Social Security fund through a flat tax called FICA. The FICA tax is about 6.2% of a person's gross paycheck. If you make more than $113K, contributions from your paycheck stop. This is called the Social Security "cap". There is a very easy way to dramatically increase revenue into the Social Security fund.

Eliminate the "cap". FICA is a flat tax on earned wages. It should be a flat tax on everyone all year regardless of the amount of earned wages. Everyone, regardless if you're in a pension plan, union or government worker you should pay into Social Security. Eliminating the "cap" would double the revenues into the Social Security trust fund. Currently the Social Security trust fund receives approximately $850 billion dollars per year. If everyone paid into the trust fund all year that amount would nearly double.

This concept is very fair. FICA is a flat tax and should be treated like a flat tax on everyone all year. If a person makes under the cap they have to pay into the Social Security trust fund all year. On the other hand if a major athlete or entertainer makes a million dollars a year they only have to pay into the fund for about 1 month of the year. For them the contributions stop. The cap on Social Security makes no sense at all.

Some may call Social Security socialism but it has been a fabric of our society for nearly 80 years. It's here to stay and it's not going away so let's strengthen for many future generations.

With this plan there is no need for "means" testing. There will be no need to increase the retirement age or reduce benefits. Besides "means" testing is unfair. As citizens we shouldn't be counting or judging each other's money or wealth. In a free country with unlimited opportunity each person can determine for themselves just how much and successful they want to be. I believe no matter how much you make or earn you should still be able to draw your fair share of Social Security.

Chapter 10

Let's pay off the National Debt

If we change the tax code to a 5% flat tax on income and eliminate the cap on Social Security the economy will explode with growth and the federal government will be awash in tax revenue. With sound fiscal budget policy in Washington there is a good chance we can eliminate the deficit and even have a surplus. If we can get the politicians to have some spending discipline we could use the surplus to begin paying off the national debt.

It's horrible the amount of national debt the U.S. currently has. This debt will be passed on to our children and grand children and reduce their standard of living. The national debt isn't just a number but the actual thing that could bring our economy and nation to its knees. With the current oppressive tax code and anemic GDP we will never be able to pay off the national debt. At the rate we're going as a nation we may never be able to balance the budget again which will only make the national debt worse. As a nation we can't sustain this debt for too much longer. At some point in the near future the crushing debt will begin to slow the economy, induce recession and possibly economic depression. When that happens there will be no money for social programs such as Social Security, Medicare, Medicaid and other forms of government welfare. No money for defense and the breakdown of social structure

People's standard of living will be greatly reduced. Investments and life savings will be wiped out. It happened before in the 1930s with the Great Depression. People went from living well in the 1920s to soup lines in the 1930s almost overnight.

Food lines of the Great Depression

Each man woman and child in the U.S. owes a share of the national debt. Last estimate was each person in the U.S. owed over $52,000 of the national debt. That's an unfair burden to place on our children and grand children if we don't do something about it soon.

If the debt keeps growing and the economy collapses, the U.S. which currently has the highest standard of living in the world could become a second or third world economy. Eventually this will become a tremendous strain and burden on all levels of government, all businesses and every citizen of this great country.

We've seen this before in the Great Depression. People lost their fortunes and everything they owned virtually overnight. In the 1920s they thought it couldn't happen but it did. It was called the roaring '20s. The attitude in the country was "let the good times roll". It started one week in October 1929 when the U.S. went from "riches to rags" in less than a year. Unemployment shot up to over 25%. People couldn't find work or feed their families. Soup kitchens popped up over night.

In 2008 it almost happened again. The U.S. came very close to depression. For a temporary time we've dodged the "depression" bullet but the growing debt has put this country into a virtual sort of flat no growth perpetual economic recession. Any type of great natural disaster or war could push this country over the economic edge. Let's face it, we have no money and we're broke as a country.

This kind of debt and economic malaise could lead to social strife or violence in the streets. A foreign power may not bring this country down but the national debt will.

Chapter 11

A new way of thinking

There is only one way out of this mess and that's a completely new and radical way of thinking. What the economy needs is **growth**. A new way of thinking to spur growth at the same time reduce the size of government and eliminate one of the most oppressive agencies, the IRS. Slashing the budget with draconian cuts will hurt the economy. Raising taxes will also hurt the economy. There is only one solution to this problem. Freeze the budget and grow the economy.

The new thinking that will grow the economy is a 5% flat tax on all forms of income and eliminating the caps on social security.

Just think about it. Here is the breakdown of federal tax receipts for FY2012.

U.S. Federal Tax Receipts – Fiscal Year 2012 ($ Billions)

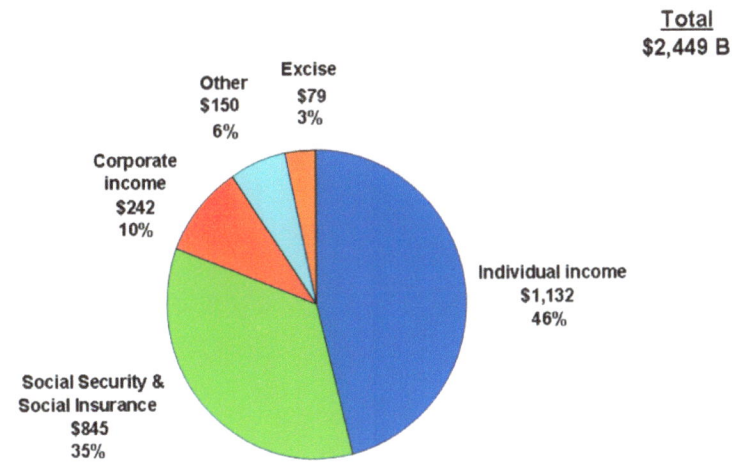

Source Data: CBO Historical Tables

With a 5% flat tax on all forms on income, individual and corporate taxes would double because of the explosive economic growth. With the caps removed, Social Security receipts into the trust fund would double. Notice in the pie chart the FY2012 U.S. federal tax receipts are $2.449 trillion dollars. If Social Security, individual income and corporate tax receipts were to double using this plan then total tax receipts would be over $4.6 trillion dollars. That's an annual surplus of $1 trillion dollars against a frozen budget of $3.5 trillion dollars. That's $1 trillion dollars that could be applied to the national debt each year thus paying it off in less than 20 years.